SPACE

Earth, Sun, and Moon

Robin Birch

CHELSEA CLUBHOUSE

Philadelphia

This edition first published in 2003 in the United States of America by Chelsea Clubhouse, a division of Chelsea House Publishers and a subsidiary of Haights Cross Communications.

Reprinted 2005

Chelsea House Publishers
2080 Cabot Boulevard West, Suite 201
Langhorne, PA 19047-1813

The Chelsea House world wide web address is www.chelseahouse.com

Library of Congress Cataloging-in-Publication Data

Birch, Robin.
    Earth, sun, and moon / by Robin Birch.
    v. cm. — (Space)
    Includes index.
    Contents: Earth — Life on Earth — Day and night — Seasons — The sun — Eclipse of the sun —
    Sunlight — Exploring the sun — The moon — The moon's shapes — Looking at the moon —
    The moon's seas and craters — People on the moon — Earth, sun, and moon facts.

    ISBN 0-7910-6970-2
    1. Earth—Juvenile literature. 2. Sun—Juvenile literature. 3. Moon—Juvenile literature.
    [1. Earth. 2. Sun. 3. Moon.] I. Title.
    QB631.4 .B57 2003
    525—dc21

                                                                        2002000037

First published in 2001 by
MACMILLAN EDUCATION AUSTRALIA PTY LTD
627 Chapel Street, South Yarra, Australia, 3141

Copyright © Robin Birch 2001
Copyright in photographs © individual photographers as credited

Edited by Carmel Heron and Louisa Kost
Cover and text design by Anne Stanhope
Illustrations by Frey Micklethwait

Printed in China

Acknowledgements

Cover photograph: View of full moon, courtesy of Photolibrary.com/John Sandford/Science Photo Library.

Photographs courtesy of: Digital Vision, p. 7; FPG International/Austral, p. 23; Getty Images, pp. 13, 14, 27; Lochman Transparencies/Bill Belson, p. 15; Lochman Transparencies/Dennis Sarson, p. 6; NASA, p. 16; NASA, supplied by Astrovisuals, pp. 12, 17, 29; Photodisc, 9, 11, 18, 21; Photo Essentials, pp. 4, 28; Photolibrary.com/John Sandford/SPL, pp. 1, 26.

While every care has been taken to trace and acknowledge copyright the publisher tenders their apologies for any accidental infringement where copyright has proved untraceable.

Contents

Earth

Earth is a **planet**. It is made mainly of rock.
It is a sphere, like a ball.

Earth's layers are the core, mantle, and crust. The core has a solid center surrounded by hot liquid. The mantle is a thicker liquid. The crust is hardened rock.

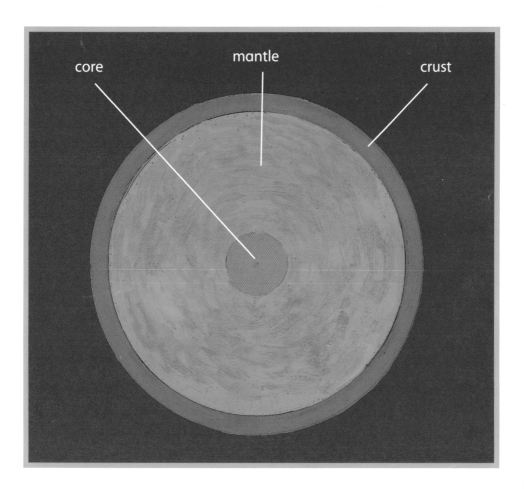

core

mantle

crust

Life on Earth

There is water on Earth's surface. A layer of gases called the atmosphere surrounds the planet. The atmosphere contains air for us to breathe. People, plants, and animals live on Earth.

Astronauts travel in **spacecraft**. They fly through Earth's atmosphere and into space. From space, astronauts can see Earth's curved shape. They see land, blue water, and white clouds.

Day and Night

Earth is spinning all the time. A day is the time it takes for Earth to spin around once. There are 24 hours in one day.

The Sun

Earth

It is daytime when your part of Earth faces the Sun. It is night when your part of Earth faces away from the Sun. From Earth, it looks like the Sun moves across the sky. But the Sun is not moving. Earth is spinning you into and away from the Sun's light.

Seasons

Earth **orbits** the Sun. A year is the time it takes Earth to travel around the Sun once. A year has 365 days.

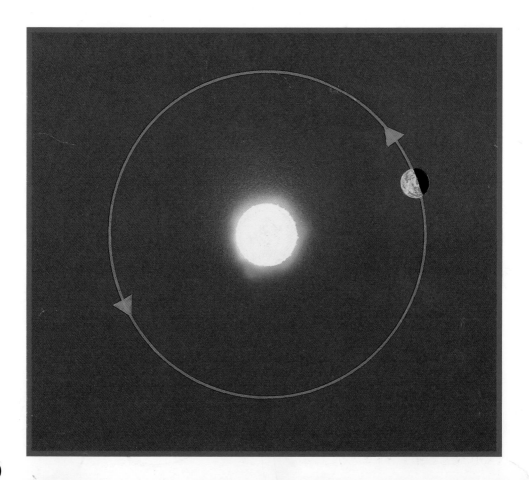

In fall, the weather becomes cooler. Some leaves change color.

The **seasons** change as Earth orbits the Sun.
The four seasons are spring, summer, fall,
and winter. It is hottest in summer and
coldest in winter.

The Sun

The Sun is a yellow star. It is the closest star to Earth. Like other stars, it is a large ball of hot, glowing gas. Looking directly at the Sun is very dangerous. It can hurt your eyes.

Eclipse of the Sun

Sometimes the Moon moves between Earth and the Sun. This event is called a **solar** eclipse. The Moon stops sunlight from reaching part of Earth. For a few minutes during the day, the sky becomes dark. We can see other stars, as if it were night.

Sunlight

Sunlight shines on Earth's atmosphere and makes the sky look blue. Sunlight also heats Earth's water. Some water turns into gas and floats into the air. The water gathers again in clouds. A rainbow appears when sunlight shines through raindrops in clouds.

Light from the Sun gives energy to plants and helps them grow. Animals and people take in this energy when they eat plants.

Exploring the Sun

In 1994, a **space probe** called *Ulysses* orbited the Sun. It sent photographs and other information back to Earth using **radio waves**. Scientists used this information to learn more about the Sun.

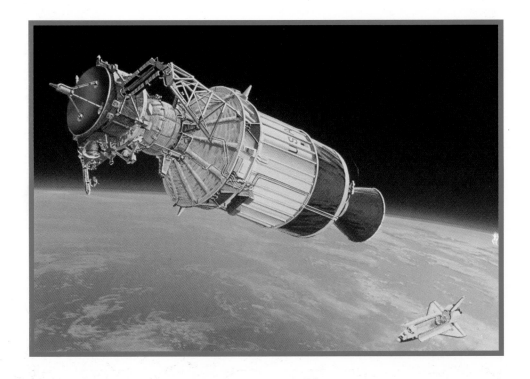

Ulysses helped scientists study rays coming from the Sun. Rays are thin beams of light. *Ulysses* also sent information about the Sun's gases, dust, and flares. A flare is a stream of gas that shoots out from the Sun.

The Moon

The Moon is also a sphere, but it is smaller than the Earth. The Moon spins slowly so the same side of it always faces Earth. This is why the surface of the Moon always looks the same.

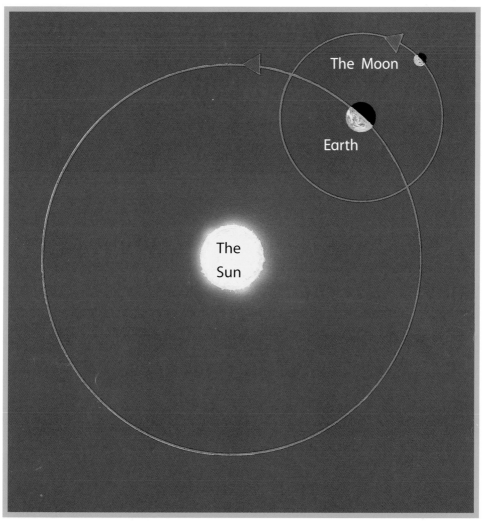

The Moon orbits Earth, and Earth orbits the Sun.

The Moon's Shapes

The Moon **reflects** light from the Sun. As the Moon travels around Earth, different parts of the Moon are lit up. This makes the Moon look as if it changes shape from day to day.

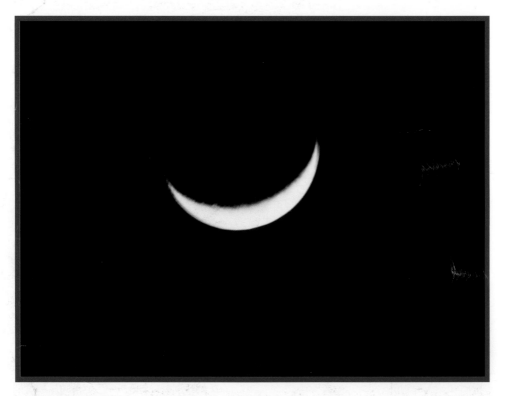

A crescent moon has a thin, curved shape.

The different shapes of the Moon are called phases. There are four main phases. They are new moon, first-quarter moon, full moon, and third-quarter moon.

new moon

first-quarter moon

full moon

third-quarter moon

Sometimes we cannot see the Moon. This is when it is located near the Sun in our sky. We cannot see the Moon reflecting sunlight in this spot. It is called a new moon.

About two weeks after a new moon, the
Moon is very bright all over. It is called a
full moon.

Looking at the Moon

The **equator** divides Earth. The half north of the equator is the northern hemisphere. The half south of the equator is the southern hemisphere.

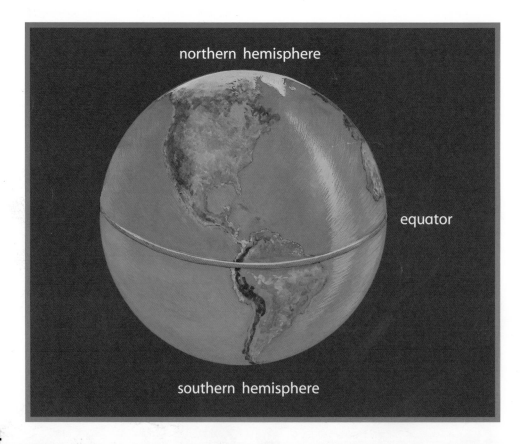

northern hemisphere

equator

southern hemisphere

The surface of the Moon has lighter and darker areas. People in the southern hemisphere see an upside-down version of the Moon that people in the northern hemisphere see.

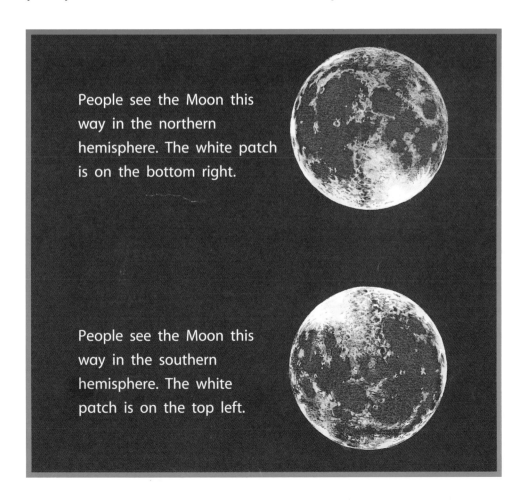

People see the Moon this way in the northern hemisphere. The white patch is on the bottom right.

People see the Moon this way in the southern hemisphere. The white patch is on the top left.

The Moon's Seas and Craters

The Moon is rocky and dusty. The darker patches we see are called seas. The seas are flat areas of rock covered with a thin layer of soil. Most of the seas are on the side of the Moon that faces Earth. The other side of the Moon has only a few seas.

The darker areas on the Moon are called seas.

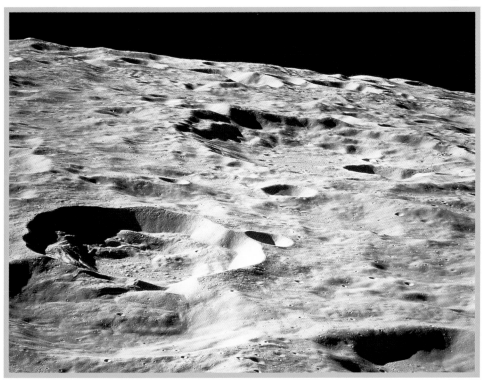

The lighter areas on the Moon are mountains.
The Moon also has **craters**. Long ago,
huge rocks crashed into the Moon, making
bowl-shaped dents. The Moon's seas were
once craters. But they filled with **lava** and
became flat when the lava cooled.

People on the Moon

Neil Armstrong and Edwin "Buzz" Aldrin were the first people to walk on the Moon. Their mission was called Apollo 11. The astronauts landed on the Moon in July 1969. They wore spacesuits to protect them from extreme temperatures. Special equipment gave them air to breathe.

On the Apollo 16 mission, astronauts landed in the mountains on the Moon. They used a moon buggy to explore the Moon's surface. They collected rocks to take back to Earth. Scientists studied these rocks to learn more about the Moon.

Earth, Sun, and Moon Facts

Earth, the Sun, and the Moon are made of different materials. They are different colors and different sizes.

	Color	Made of	Size (distance across)
Earth	blue and white	rock	7,927 miles (12,756 kilometers)
Sun	yellow	gas	864,367 miles (1,391,000 kilometers)
Moon	gray	rock	2,160 miles (3,476 kilometers)

Glossary

astronaut   a person trained to travel and work in space

crater   a bowl-shaped hole in the ground

equator   an imaginary line that divides Earth into a northern hemisphere and a southern hemisphere

lava   very hot, melted rock that flows up from the center of a planet or moon

orbit   to circle an object in space; also, the path that a planet or moon takes when circling another object in space.

planet   a huge ball of rock or gas in space; nine planets orbit the Sun in our solar system.

radio waves   invisible rays that can carry information

reflect   to turn back; the Moon reflects light from the Sun.

season   a period of time each year with a certain kind of weather; the four seasons are spring, summer, fall, and winter.

solar   having to do with the Sun

spacecraft   a vehicle that moves through space

space probe   a spacecraft that explores space and does not carry people; space probes are controlled by people on Earth.

Index